P9-BYZ-750

casseroles

tessa bramley

PHOTOGRAPHY BY CRAIG ROBERTSON

casseroles
COMFORT FOOD AT ITS BEST

RYLAND
PETERS
& SMALL

LONDON NEW YORK

Senior Designer	Paul Tilby
Editor	Maddalena Bastianelli
Production	Meryl Silbert
Art Director	Gabriella Le Grazie
Publishing Director	Alison Starling
Food Stylist	Tessa Bramley
Stylist	Helen Trent

AUTHOR ACKNOWLEDGMENTS

This book would not have been possible without the commitment and hard work of my staff at the Old Vicarage. My thanks, in particular, to Nathan and Andrew for backing me in all that I do and for testing the recipes. Their good humor and technical skills have been invaluable—as always! Thanks also to Andrew and Carole (my son and daughter-in-law), for their inspiration and for selflessly eating their way through every dish. Many thanks to Mum, Howard, and Linda for their support and continuous belief in me. Finally, I am indebted to my agent Fiona at Limelight and to the team at Ryland Peters & Small; especially Maddie for her endless patience with words, Paul for his beautiful design, and Craig for his stunning photography. Thank you guys!

First published in the United States in 2000
by Ryland Peters & Small Inc.,
150th West 56th Street, Suite 6303
New York, NY 10019

Text © Tessa Bramley 2000
Design and photographs © Ryland Peters & Small 2000

10 9 8 7 6 5 4 3 2 1

Printed and bound in China by Toppan Printing Co.

ISBN 1 84172 098 4

A catalog record for this book is available from the Library of Congress.

Notes

All spoon measurements are level unless otherwise stated.

All fruits and vegetables should be washed thoroughly and peeled, unless otherwise stated. Unwaxed citrus fruits should be used whenever possible.

Specialty Asian ingredients are available in large supermarkets and Thai, Chinese, and other Asian stores.

CONTENTS

A brief sauté followed by relaxed, gentle cooking in a moderate oven will melt tough meat fibers into tender sweetness. Casseroles, braises, and pot-roasts are the convenience meals of today. They can be assembled quickly and ahead of time, are often marinated with herbs and aromatics for extra flavor, then left to cook undisturbed. This is delicious, comforting home-cooked food at its best.

INTRODUCTION

As a child, I remember my grandmother cooking wonderful slow-cooked meals. Her pot-roasts and casseroles would fill the whole house with delicious meaty aromas. Real home-cooking, using the best local ingredients and home-grown produce, is what I grew up on.

Casseroling is a simple, foolproof cooking technique. In fact, it's almost impossible for you to go wrong. First of all choose an ovenproof casserole with a tight-fitting lid. The size of the dish will depend on what you are cooking and for how many people, but in general, do not fill the casserole more than two-thirds full. A flameproof casserole is better still. As most recipes require you to brown vegetables or sear meat in hot oil or butter first (to add color and flavor), you can save time—and cleaning up—if this can be done in the same cookware that will transfer to the oven. However, a heavy-bottom skillet is just as good for browning and searing. It is useful—and fun—to have a selection of casserole dishes to fit the contents as well as the occasion.

Homemade stock will always give your casserole the best flavor. Try to get into the habit of making your own, then you can refrigerate or freeze it until needed.

Put the carcass of birds, meat, or fish bones in a large stockpot or saucepan, add vegetables, such as carrots, onions, and celery, and fill with cold water. Throw in some fresh herbs, if using, and freshly cracked black pepper. Boil, then simmer. Skim off the solids that rise to the surface. For chicken and meat stocks, simmer for 1 hour, but simmer fish stock for 20 minutes only or it will become bitter. Strain before using. Supermarkets now sell tubs of fresh stock, so you could use this if you don't have time to make your own. Use the appropriate stock for the kind of meat you are cooking: chicken for chicken casseroles, beef for beef dishes, and so on. Wine adds flavor too. In general, use a full-bodied red wine for dark meat and a robust, dry white wine for white meat and fish.

Flavors develop, concentrate, and meld together in a moist-cooking medium when ingredients are casseroled, pot-roasted, or braised. Long, slow-cooking tenderizes meat, so less expensive, tougher cuts can be used. The connective tissue in the meat melts into the cooking liquid to give a thick, juicy sauce. To finish, creamy mashed potatoes, fluffy rice, or crusty country-style bread are all you need to complete a hearty meal.

OVEN-BAKED CHOWDER

This chunky fish and vegetable stew often includes salt pork and potatoes. Some recipes call for tomatoes or corn as well. In Brittany, soups are cooked in a pot called a *chaudière*, and maybe the name chowder was derived from this. Chowders are a speciality of New England, where they are often made with shellfish, particularly clams. I like to make mine with Manila clams, which are much sweeter and more tender than the larger varieties. This one-pot meal is easy to make and perfect for a warming supper served with crusty bread.

Put the salt pork or bacon in a large, deep skillet and sauté until crisp and golden. Remove to a plate. Add the onion and celery root to the bacon fat in the pan and cook until browned. Remove to a plate.

Blanch the potatoes in salted boiling water for 1 minute, then drain. Heat the butter in the skillet, add the flour, and cook, stirring for 1 minute. Gradually add the hot milk, beating until the sauce is smooth and thickened. Add the potatoes, sautéed vegetables, and 2 cups water. Mix well, then pour into a casserole. Stir in the corn.

Cover and cook in a preheated oven at 350°F for about 1 hour until the vegetables are soft and start to fall apart. Remove from the oven, add the cod or haddock, cover, and let stand for a few minutes: the heat of the stew will cook the fish.

Meanwhile, put the clams or mussels in a roasting pan and put in the oven for 2-3 minutes until the shells open. Discard any that have not opened. Remove the shellfish and strain any juices left in the shells. Add the shellfish, juices, cream, and nutmeg to the chowder and stir gently to mix. Heat through and add salt and pepper to taste. Ladle into 4 deep dishes and serve with chopped chives or parsley.

7 oz. rindless salt pork or slab bacon, diced

2 onions, finely chopped

1 celery root, about 1 lb., finely chopped

2 tablespoons unsalted butter

1 tablespoon flour

2 cups hot milk

2 medium potatoes, diced

1/2 cup fresh or frozen corn kernels

1 lb. cod or haddock fillet, skinned, boned, and cut into large chunks

2 lb. clams or mussels, cleaned

2/3 cup heavy cream

1/4 teaspoon freshly grated nutmeg

sea salt and freshly ground black pepper

chopped fresh chives or parsley, to serve

SERVES 4

FISH and SHELLFISH

This traditional Scottish stew—known as *Cullen Skink*—is made with smoked Finnan haddock, thickened with potatoes, and enriched with a splash of cream. If you can't get this fish, use a naturally smoked haddock or whitefish instead. Don't use the bright yellow variety as this is artificially colored and does not have such a good flavor.

SMOKED HADDOCK STEW
with potatoes and celery root

Heat the butter in a large saucepan, add the onions, potatoes, and celery root, and cook, stirring, until softened. Add the fish stock, 1 cup water, and pepper. Bring to a boil, then pour into a casserole.

Cover and cook in a preheated oven at 300°F for 50 minutes or until the potatoes and celery root have disintegrated into the liquid and the mixture has thickened. Remove from the oven.

Pour the milk into the casserole. Put the smoked haddock or whitefish, skin side up, on top of the vegetables and return to the oven for a further 4-5 minutes until the fish is cooked and opaque. Remove from the oven and take out the haddock or whitefish. Peel off and discard the skin and bones. Flake the fish with a fork and set aside.

Stir the cream into the casserole and reheat. Return the fish to the casserole, then serve in deep dishes with the chopped parsley.

VARIATION:

For a smoother soup-stew, after removing the fish from the casserole, press the remaining mixture through a coarse strainer. Proceed with the recipe and add extra milk or cream, if necessary.

2 tablespoons unsalted butter

2 onions, finely chopped

2 medium potatoes, diced

1 celery root, about 1 lb., finely chopped

1 cup fish stock

2 cups hot milk

2 lb. undyed smoked haddock, preferably finnan haddie

about ⅔ cup heavy cream

a large handful of fresh parsley, chopped, to serve

sea salt and freshly ground black pepper

SERVES 4

Monkfish is a meaty fish that's ideal for casseroling, with the juices in the pot keeping it moist. Rubbed with this wonderful spice mix, the fish can be left for up to 2 hours for the flavors to intensify. I like to rub thickly sliced French bread with garlic and olive oil, pop it in on a tray, and put it in the oven to crisp. It's delicious with the fish.

CUMIN and CORIANDER SPICED MONKFISH with chiles

Heat 2 tablespoons of the oil in a skillet, add the leeks and celery root, and cook until just golden. Transfer to a casserole and season with salt and pepper. Dry-roast the spice seeds in a nonstick skillet for 2 minutes to release the aromas. Let cool, lightly crush with a mortar and pestle, then rub half onto the monkfish and refrigerate until needed.

Heat 2 tablespoons of the oil in the skillet, add the shallots or onions, chiles, and garlic, and sauté until just softened. Add the remaining spice mix and mix well. Add the saffron and a few tablespoons of the wine. Cook briefly until the color and flavor emerge from the saffron. Season lightly. Pour in the remaining wine, bring to a boil, and add to the casserole. Cover and cook in a preheated oven at 350°F for 30 minutes until softened.

Heat the remaining oil in a nonstick skillet and lightly brown the fish on one side. Put it on top of the vegetables in the casserole and surround it with the zucchini. Season lightly.

Return to the oven and cook uncovered for 10 minutes until the fish is cooked and the zucchini are bright green. Using a slotted spoon, transfer the fish and vegetables to a deep dish and keep them warm.

Strain the cooking liquid into a saucepan and bring to a boil. Add the cream and cook until reduced and thickened. Pour the sauce over the fish and vegetables and serve with the chopped cilantro.

6 tablespoons olive oil

3 leeks, trimmed and thickly sliced

1 celery root, about 1 lb., cut into large chunks

4 teaspoons cumin seeds

4 teaspoons coriander seeds

black seeds from 18 green cardamom pods, crushed

6 shallots or 2 small onions, finely chopped

3 green medium hot chiles, seeded and finely sliced

3 fat garlic cloves, finely sliced

1 large pinch of saffron threads

3 cups dry white wine

2 monkfish fillets, about 1 lb. each, skinned, boned, and cut in half

3 medium zucchini, sliced diagonally

1 cup heavy cream

a large handful of fresh cilantro, chopped

salt and freshly ground mixed peppercorns

SERVES 4

Lift the small fillet on the underside of each chicken breast and insert a sage leaf. Season with salt and pepper and set aside. Peel and trim the vegetables, then cut into even-sized chunks, but leave the shallots whole. Set aside.

Heat the stock in a large saucepan until boiling. Add the chicken thighs and legs, reduce the heat, and simmer for about 20 minutes. Drain, reserving the stock.

Put the chicken breasts, carrots, and parsnips in a large, shallow, ovenproof dish. Add 2–3 sprigs of the sage and the thyme. Season with salt and pepper. Add the partially cooked chicken thighs and legs and enough hot stock to cover. Cook, covered, in a preheated oven at 350°F for about 45 minutes or until the juices run clear when a chicken thigh is pierced with a skewer.

Remove from the oven. Using a slotted spoon, take out the chicken pieces and half the vegetables and keep them warm.

Put the remaining vegetables and cooking liquid in a food processor or blender and purée until smooth. Strain into a large saucepan. Chop the remaining sage and add to the pan with the cream. Heat until the sauce has reduced and thickened slightly. Season to taste.

Return the chicken and vegetables to the dish, add the leeks, and pour over the sauce. Cook for a further 20–25 minutes until the chicken is cooked and the vegetables are golden and glazed. Serve with sage leaves or flowers, if using, and buttered cabbage.

4 lb. small chicken pieces, including breasts, thighs, and legs, preferably free-range

7–8 sprigs of sage

6 carrots

4 small thin leeks

4 parsnips

16 shallots

7 cups chicken stock

3–4 sprigs of thyme

$2/3$ cup heavy cream

salt and freshly ground black pepper

sage leaves or flowers, to serve (optional)

SERVES 4

CHICKEN, SAGE, and PARSNIP CASSEROLE

With bold, gutsy flavors and a surprisingly silky sauce, this dish won't fail to impress. It's perfect for an elegant dinner party and is made even more stylish if scattered with sage flowers.

POULTRY AND GAME

Lift the skin of the chicken pieces and tuck a few tarragon leaves between the skin and flesh. Season with salt and freshly ground black pepper.

Using a sharp knife, cut long strips of zest from the lemons (leaving the bitter white pith). Squeeze the lemons and reserve the juice. Blanch a strip of peel in boiling water, remove, and plunge into ice water to cool. When cold, cut into fine shreds and reserve.

Heat half the butter in a heavy-bottom skillet until foaming, then add the chicken pieces, and brown on all sides. Transfer to a casserole and add the strips of lemon zest .

Heat the remaining butter in the same skillet, add the onion and saffron threads, and sauté until the onion is softened. Add the lemon juice and sugar, if using, and bring to a boil. Add the stock and return to a boil. Stir in half the cream, salt, and pepper, then add to the casserole. Cover with a lid.

To make the tarragon potatoes, put the potatoes on a sheet of heavy-duty aluminum foil, add the butter, tarragon, and salt. Bring the edges of the foil together and scrunch to seal.

Cook the casserole and potatoes in a preheated oven at 350°F for about 1–1½ hours, or until cooked. To test if the chicken is done, pierce the thickest part of a chicken thigh with a skewer—the juices should run clear. If not, cook for 10 minutes more, then test again. Remove the chicken and potatoes and keep them warm.

Pour the cooking liquid into a saucepan. Discard the lemon zest. Add the remaining cream and heat until reduced and caramelized. Add salt and pepper to taste.

Put the chicken on a serving plate, pour over the sauce, and top with the reserved lemon shreds and remaining tarragon. Serve with the tarragon potatoes.

POT-ROASTED CHICKEN
with saffron and lemon

A light chicken casserole, combining the freshness of lemon with the heady scent and color of saffron. Scatter with a handful of tarragon leaves and serve with foil-baked buttery potatoes for a fresh spring treat.

4 lb. small chicken pieces, including breasts, thighs, and legs, preferably free-range

a handful of fresh tarragon leaves

2 small, thin-skinned unwaxed lemons

1 onion, finely chopped

2 large pinches of saffron threads

1 tablespoon sugar (optional)

2 cups chicken stock

¼ cup unsalted butter

1 cup heavy cream

sea salt and freshly ground black pepper

TARRAGON POTATOES:

1 lb. small new potatoes, scrubbed

¼ cup unsalted butter

a handful of fresh tarragon leaves

sea salt

SERVES 4

In the north of England and Scotland, pearl barley is used to thicken and enrich soups, broths, and stews; it was certainly one of my grandmother's favorites. The long, slow cooking of this broth means the chicken will be meltingly tender and will literally fall off the bone. Comforting and warming, it is perfect on a cold, windy night. Pheasant or rabbit can be used for a richer, darker broth.

CHICKEN BROTH with pearl barley and rosemary

2 tablespoons unsalted butter

4 lb. small chicken pieces, including breasts, thighs, and legs, preferably free-range

1 onion, finely chopped

2 carrots, diced

2 leeks, diced

2 celery stalks, diced

1 cup red wine

2 fresh bay leaves

1 sprig of rosemary

8 juniper berries, crushed

1/4 cup pearl barley

2 medium potatoes, diced

8 cups chicken stock

sea salt and freshly ground black pepper

TO SERVE: (optional)

chopped fresh parsley or chives

sour cream

SERVES 4

Heat half the butter in a large skillet, add the chicken pieces, and sauté until browned on all sides. Remove and put in a deep casserole. Season lightly with salt and freshly ground black pepper.

Add the remaining butter to the skillet, add the onion, carrots, leeks, and celery, and cook until softened and the butter has been absorbed. Transfer to the casserole.

Put the wine, bay leaves, rosemary, juniper berries, salt, and pepper in a saucepan and bring to a boil. Pour into the casserole. Put the pearl barley, potatoes, and stock in the skillet, bring to a boil, and add to the casserole.

Cover and cook in a preheated oven at 325°F for about 1 hour, then reduce to 300°F and cook, uncovered, for a further 1-1½ hours until thickened.

Remove and discard the bay leaves and rosemary and add salt and pepper, to taste. To serve, ladle the broth into heated, deep, soup plates, sprinkle with chopped parsley or chives, and add a swirl of sour cream, if using.

We all have a favorite recipe for *coq au vin*, so I thought it would be interesting to use a gutsy white wine instead of the traditional red. The prunes add extra richness and flavor, but you can omit them if you want to. *Coq au vin rouge* it's not, but delicious nonetheless.

COQ AU VIN BLANC

¹/₄ cup olive oil

¹/₂ cup diced pancetta or slab bacon

20 shallots, 4 finely chopped and 16 left whole

2 garlic cloves, finely chopped

¹/₄ cup unsalted butter

2¹/₄ cups button mushrooms

2 tablespoons flour

8 chicken quarters

2 bay leaves

4–5 sprigs of thyme

4–5 sprigs of parsley

12 prunes, pitted

2 cups full-bodied, dry white wine

1 cup chicken stock

2 tablespoons Amontillado or other medium dry sherry

sea salt and freshly ground mixed peppercorns

SERVES 4

Heat 1 tablespoon of the oil in a deep skillet, add the pancetta or bacon, and sauté until crisp. Remove with a slotted spoon and set aside. Add the chopped shallots and garlic to the bacon fat in the skillet and sauté until lightly golden. Remove and set aside.

Heat half the butter and 1 tablespoon of the oil in the skillet, add the whole shallots and mushrooms, and sauté until lightly golden. Remove and set aside.

Season the flour with salt and pepper, then toss the chicken pieces in it until lightly coated. Heat the remaining oil in the same skillet, add the chicken, and sauté until golden (cook in batches, if necessary). Put the chicken and vegetables in a casserole. Tuck in the bay leaves and add the thyme, parsley, and prunes. Season.

Heat the wine and stock in saucepan until just boiling, then pour it over the chicken and vegetables. Cover and cook in a preheated oven at 350°F for about 1½ hours or until the chicken is done. To test, pierce the thickest part of a thigh with a skewer—the juices should run clear. If not, cook for about 10 minutes more and test again.

Remove the chicken and vegetables and keep them hot. Strain the cooking liquid and reserve. Heat the sherry in a saucepan until reduced by half—this will burn off some of the alcohol and concentrate the flavor. Add the reserved liquid, return to a boil, and cook until reduced by half.

Beat in the remaining butter, in small pieces, to thicken the sauce and give it a glossy finish.

Serve the chicken and vegetables with the sauce poured over.

Using a sharp knife, make small incisions in the turkey rolls and insert the garlic slivers and cilantro.

Melt the butter in a heavy-bottom skillet until foaming, then add the turkey, and sear until golden on all sides. Remove and put into a casserole.

Add the onion, chopped garlic, and chiles to the skillet and cook until softened. Transfer to the casserole. Put the wine into the skillet, bring to a boil, and cook until reduced by half. Add the stock and return to a boil.

Remove and discard the outer layer of the lemongrass, then crush the stems with a rolling pin or knife to release the flavor. Add to the skillet.

Add the coconut milk, return to a boil, and season. Pour over the turkey and vegetables and cook, uncovered, in a preheated oven at 400°F for about 20 minutes. Cover, reduce to 350°F, and cook for a further 1½ hours until tender. For the last 15 minutes of cooking, remove the lid and increase to 400°F to brown the turkey.

Slice the turkey and serve with the sauce, Thai fragrant rice, and cilantro.

2 turkey thighs, boned, rolled, and tied (ask your butcher to do this)

4 fat garlic cloves, 2 cut into slivers and 2 finely chopped

a handful of fresh cilantro

2 tablespoons unsalted butter

1 onion, finely chopped

3 hot red chiles, seeded and finely sliced into rings

1 cup white wine

1 cup turkey or chicken stock

2 stalks lemongrass

1½ cups unsweetened coconut milk

sea salt and freshly ground mixed peppercorns

TO SERVE:

Thai fragrant rice

a handful of fresh cilantro

SERVES 4

Turkey thighs are relatively inexpensive. The dark meat has a richer flavor than the lighter breast meat—and it is a perfect match for the distinctive flavors of Thai cooking.

BRAISED TURKEY
with coconut and lemongrass

CASSEROLED DUCK with fresh figs

Sweet, dark-purple figs will counterbalance the richness of duck. Make sure they are completely ripe for the best flavor.

Remove the skin from the duck breasts. Heat a heavy-bottom skillet, add the skins, and fry until the fat melts. Discard the skins but reserve the fat. Meanwhile, lift the small fillet on the underside of each breast and insert a few sage leaves. Season all the duck pieces.

Add the onion, celery, and leeks to the duck fat in the skillet and sauté until lightly golden. Transfer to an ovenproof, flameproof dish or roasting pan. Add the sherry to the skillet and heat, stirring, until reduced to a sticky glaze. Pour in the wine, bring to a boil, and cook until reduced by half. Add the stock, return to a boil, and pour on top of the vegetables. Add the chopped figs, then top with the duck legs, skin side up.

Cook, uncovered, in a preheated oven at 350°F for about 1–1½ hours, basting the duck from time to time with the pan juices.

Blanch the remaining leeks in boiling salted water for 1 minute to soften, then drain and add to the baking dish. Lay the duck breasts on top of the vegetables and baste with the juices. Cook, uncovered, for a further 10–12 minutes until the legs are well done, the skin is crispy, and the breasts still slightly pink. Remove the duck and the pieces of leek and keep them hot.

To make the sauce, strain the cooking liquid into a saucepan, pressing the vegetables and figs through the strainer with the back of a wooden spoon to extract all the flavor. Cook over a high heat until slightly thickened. To finish, beat in the butter, a little at a time, until the sauce is glossy and thick. Season to taste. Add the fig quarters and heat through.

Put the duck, leeks, and figs into a deep serving plate, pour over the sauce, and serve—fabulous!

8 pieces (breasts and legs) of lean duck, about 8 oz. each

5–6 sprigs of sage

1 onion, chopped

2 celery stalks, chopped

3 leeks, 1 chopped and 2 cut into 1-inch pieces

¼ cup Amontillado or other medium dry sherry

1 cup full-bodied red wine

3 cups duck or chicken stock

8 fresh figs, 4 coarsely chopped and 4 quartered

2 tablespoons unsalted butter

sea salt and freshly ground black pepper

SERVES 4

Season the duck pieces with salt and pepper. Using a sharp knife, make 2–3 shallow, diagonal cuts in the duck breasts.

Heat a cast-iron skillet and dry-fry the breasts, skin side down, until the fat melts and the skin is crisp and golden. Remove and set aside.

Add the onion, garlic, potatoes, and celery root to the duck fat in the skillet and sauté until golden. (Add a little of the butter, if necessary.) Transfer to the casserole. Put the duck thighs in the skillet, sauté until golden, then add to the casserole. Tuck in the sprigs of rosemary.

Pour the port into the skillet and heat, stirring to de-glaze the pan juices. Cook until reduced by half. Add the wine, return to a boil, and reduce again by half. Pour it over the vegetables and duck thighs. Heat the stock until boiling, then add to the casserole. Cover and cook in a preheated oven at 350°F for 1 hour.

Reserve 1 tablespoon of the blueberries, then put the rest in a small saucepan, add the sugar, and cook until the fruit is soft and pulpy. Push through a strainer to remove the seeds and give a deep red purée.

Remove the casserole from the oven, add the partially cooked breasts, skin side up, and stir in the fruit purée. Increase to 400°F and cook, uncovered, for 20–25 minutes until the duck thighs are meltingly tender and the breasts crisp but still slightly pink. Using a slotted spoon, remove the vegetables and duck pieces to a heated serving dish and keep them warm. Remove and discard the rosemary sprigs. Add the reserved blueberries.

Pour the cooking liquid into a saucepan, add salt and pepper, and bring to a boil. If you prefer a thicker sauce, beat in the butter—a little at a time—until glossy and slightly thickened. Pour the sauce over the duck and serve with buttered spinach.

8 pieces of lean duck, including breasts and thighs, about 8 oz. each

1 red onion, chopped

2 garlic cloves, finely chopped

3 medium potatoes, cut into chunks

1 celery root, about 1 lb., cut into chunks

2 tablespoons unsalted butter (optional)

2 sprigs of rosemary

$^2/_3$ cup ruby port

$^2/_3$ cup red wine

1 cup duck or chicken stock

1 cup blueberries

1 tablespoon sugar

sea salt and freshly ground black pepper

SERVES 4

DUCK with blueberries and rosemary

You can make your own duck stock using duck bones and drumsticks. Blueberries complement the rich flavor of duck, but you can also use blackberries when in season.

The bacon jacket protects the guinea fowl, keeping it moist and succulent while cooking. Try to use free-range birds if you can as they have the best flavor. For a crispy bacon wrapping, cook in a shallow, ovenproof gratin dish.

GUINEA FOWL WRAPPED in BACON
with cinnamon and port

2 guinea fowl or game hens, about 2½ lb. each, cut into 4 breast and 4 leg portions

5–6 sprigs of thyme

8 thin slices pancetta or bacon

2–3 tablespoons olive oil

1 celery root, about 1 lb., cut into medium chunks

2 red onions, cut into quarters

8 small carrots, peeled and left whole

⅔ cup tawny port

2 cups chicken stock

3 cups full-bodied red wine, such as Rhône

3 bay leaves

1 large cinnamon stick, broken into 3–4 pieces

1 tablespoon unsalted butter

1 tablespoon large green olives, rinsed and pitted

sea salt and freshly ground black pepper

SERVES 4

Lift the skin of each piece of guinea fowl, tuck up a few sprigs of the thyme, then season and wrap with the pancetta or bacon. Tie with kitchen string.

Heat the oil in a skillet, add the bacon-wrapped guinea fowl, and sear until browned on all sides. Remove to an ovenproof dish. Add the vegetables to the skillet, sauté until lightly golden, then transfer to the dish.

Pour the port and stock into the skillet and heat, stirring, to dissolve the pan juices. Add to the dish. Put the wine in the skillet and cook until reduced by a third. Add the bay leaves, cinnamon, and the remaining thyme and pour over the guinea fowl.

Cover and cook in a preheated oven at 350°F for about 30 minutes, then remove the breasts and vegetables and keep them warm. Baste the legs, cover, return to the oven, and bake for a further 35-45 minutes until cooked. Pierce the thickest part of a thigh with a skewer—the juices should run clear. Put the breasts and vegetables back into the dish and return to the oven until golden.

Remove the guinea fowl and vegetables to a serving dish and strain the cooking liquid into a saucepan. Bring to a boil, then beat in the butter—a little at a time—until the sauce is thick and glossy. Add the olives and heat through.

To serve, pour the sauce over the guinea fowl and vegetables and serve with mashed parsnips and buttered cabbage.

SLOW-COOKED PORK RIBS
with tamarind and star anise

Star anise, a sweet spice with an aniseed flavor, is used in Chinese cooking. Here, it marinates into the pork to increase the meat's natural sweetness, while the tamarind adds a pleasing sour note to the dish. The apples help to thicken the sweet-and-sour sauce.

3 lb. pork ribs in one piece, about 8 ribs

2 tablespoons seasoned flour

2 tablespoons unsalted butter

2 onions or 6 shallots, finely chopped

2 celery stalks, finely sliced

2 small apples, peeled, cored, and coarsely chopped

²/₃ cup Madeira wine

3 cups light, fruity red wine, such as Beaujolais

5 cups pork or chicken stock

sea salt and freshly ground black pepper

TO SERVE:

chopped fresh cilantro (optional)

Thai fragrant rice

MARINADE:

4 garlic cloves, crushed

2 teaspoons tamarind paste* or 1 tablespoon fresh lemon juice

5 star anise, broken into pieces

1 teaspoon black peppercorns, crushed

2 bay leaves, torn

3 tablespoons red wine vinegar

a handful of fresh cilantro

¼ cup olive oil

Note: Tamarind paste is available from Asian markets or larger supermarkets.

SERVES 4

To make the marinade, put all the ingredients in a bowl and mix well. Rub it into the pork, then cover and let marinate in the fridge for several hours.

Take the pork out of the marinade and pat it dry with paper towels. Toss in the seasoned flour and shake off any excess. Reserve the marinade.

Melt half the butter in a heavy-bottom skillet. Add the pork and sear until browned on all sides. Put in a deep casserole.

Heat the remaining butter in the same skillet, add the onions or shallots, celery, and apples, and sauté until golden. Transfer to the casserole. Stir the Madeira and half the wine into the skillet and heat, stirring to dissolve all the sticky sediment. Add the rest of the wine, boil until slightly thickened, then pour into the casserole. Heat the reserved marinade and the stock and add to the casserole.

Cover and cook in a preheated oven at 300°F for about 1 hour, then lower to 250°F for a further 3–3½ hours, adding water or more stock, as necessary. Take care that it doesn't boil dry. When the pork is tender, remove from the oven, let cool, and chill overnight.

The next day, remove and discard the solidified fat from the surface, then reheat the dish thoroughly. Season to taste.

To serve, slice the pork into ribs, spoon the sauce over the top, and sprinkle with chopped cilantro, if using. Serve with Thai fragrant rice.

Using a sharp knife or apple corer, make a cavity through the length of the pork. Stuff with the prunes and marjoram. Season with salt and pepper. Heat 2 tablespoons of the oil in a heavy-bottom cast-iron skillet, add the pork, and sear until browned on all sides. Remove and set aside.

Heat the remaining oil in the skillet, add the onion and garlic, and sauté until softened and translucent. Stir in the cabbage and apples, mix well, then add the sherry and vinegar. Bring to a boil, reduce the heat, add the sugar, and stir until dissolved. Season and add the nutmeg and cinnamon sticks. Transfer to a large, deep casserole, top with the pork, and add about ⅔ cup of the hot stock.

Cook, uncovered, in a preheated oven at 400°F for 30 minutes, then reduce to 325°F, cover, and cook for 1½ hours, adding more stock as necessary. Remove from the oven. The cabbage should be tender and moist and the pork meltingly tender with juices running clear. Take out and discard the cinnamon.

Slice the pork and put it on top of the red cabbage. Serve with mashed potatoes and fried apple rings.

Pork shoulder used to be quite fatty, so it was traditionally slow-cooked with fruits and sweet vegetables. Today, pork is much leaner but it is still delicious cooked this way. If you're not a fan of prunes, leave them out and stud the pork with garlic and marjoram instead. Season the cabbage well to bring out its full flavor.

BRAISED PORK
with prunes and red cabbage

4 lb. boned and rolled shoulder of pork, rind and excess fat removed

14 prunes, pitted

3–4 sprigs of marjoram

¼ cup olive oil

1 large onion, finely chopped

1 garlic clove, finely chopped

1 small red cabbage, about 1 lb., halved, central core removed, and leaves finely sliced

3 eating apples*, peeled, cored, and cut into small cubes

2 tablespoons Amontillado or other medium dry sherry

2 tablespoons red wine vinegar

3 tablespoons brown sugar

¼ teaspoon freshly grated nutmeg

2 cinnamon sticks, broken into pieces

2 cups hot pork or chicken stock

sea salt and freshly ground black pepper

*Note: Use firm apples which hold their shape during cooking.

SERVES 4

1 cup dried lima beans or
14 oz. canned lima beans

¾ cup dried cannellini beans or
14 oz. canned cannellini beans

1 cup fresh or frozen fava beans

20 fat garlic cloves, 18 whole,
2 cut into slivers

⅔ cup milk

2 tablespoons unsalted butter

2 onions, finely chopped

2 celery stalks, finely sliced

1 tablespoon juniper berries,
crushed

1 sprig of thyme

2 cups pork or chicken stock

3 lb. loin of pork, skinned

5-6 fresh sage leaves, torn

sea salt and freshly ground
black pepper

chopped flat-leaf parsley, to
serve

HONEY AND MUSTARD
GLAZE:

1 tablespoon dry mustard

1 tablespoon whole-grain mustard

5 tablespoons soft cider

2 tablespoons olive oil

2 teaspoons honey

SERVES 4

The aromatic, meaty juices from the pork soak into the beans, keeping them creamy and full of flavor. You can also use boned and rolled shoulder of pork, which is less expensive, but it will take an hour longer to cook.

HONEY and MUSTARD GLAZED PORK
with beans, garlic, and juniper

If using dried beans, soak them overnight in cold water to cover, then drain and rinse. Rub off their skins with your fingertips (a simple but tedious job) and put the beans into a saucepan. Add cold water, bring to a boil, then simmer and cook for 5 minutes. Do not salt the water or the beans will be tough. If using canned beans, drain and rinse.

Blanch the fava beans in boiling water for about 1 minute, drain, then put into a bowl of chilled water to retain their bright green color. Slip the beans out of their gray skins and discard the skins.

Put the whole garlic cloves in a saucepan, add the milk, and heat until just boiling. Remove from the heat and let stand to infuse.

Melt the butter in a large skillet, add the onion, celery, and juniper berries, and sauté until softened and translucent. Add the lima and cannellini beans, the whole garlic cloves and the infused milk, thyme, and about 1½ cups of the stock. Bring to a boil. Transfer to a casserole, cover, and put in a preheated oven at 350°F while you prepare the pork.

To make the glaze, mix all the ingredients together in a bowl. Using a sharp knife, make small incisions in the pork and insert the garlic slivers and sage leaves. Season with salt and pepper. Heat a skillet until hot, add the pork, and dry-fry until golden on all sides. Remove and brush with the honey and mustard glaze to coat. Add to the casserole.

Cover and cook for about 1¾ hours until the beans are tender and creamy and the meat is tender, but still juicy. Check during cooking and if it looks dry, add the remaining stock.

Remove the thyme, stir in the fava beans, then add salt and pepper. Increase to 400°F. Return to the oven and cook uncovered for 20-25 minutes until the pork has browned and the beans are cooked.

To serve, spoon the beans into heated, deep dishes, top with slices of the pork, and sprinkle with lots of chopped parsley.

My grandmother used to make the best braised oxtail ever, so I thought I'd adapt her recipe to use sparerib chops. It's deliciously rich and sticky—and perfect with nutmeg mashed potatoes and braised root vegetables (see page 53).

BRAISED RIB CHOPS in RED WINE
with cinnamon and orange

8 pork rib chops, about 1½ inches thick

2 tablespoons seasoned flour

¼ cup olive oil

1 red onion, chopped

2 celery stalks, chopped

2 carrots, cut into medium cubes

⅔ cup ruby port

3 cups full-bodied red wine

5 cups beef stock

3 cinnamon sticks

3 bay leaves

1 teaspoon black peppercorns, crushed

5–6 sprigs of thyme

zest of 1 orange, removed in long strips

sea salt and freshly ground black pepper

SERVES 4

Toss the rib chops in the seasoned flour until coated, shaking off any excess flour.

Heat half the oil in a large, heavy-bottom skillet, add the ribs, and sear until browned on all sides. Transfer to a deep casserole.

Heat the remaining oil in the same skillet, add the onion, celery, and carrots, and sauté until golden. Add to the casserole.

Stir the port into the skillet and heat, stirring to dissolve the sediment. Reduce until sticky. Add the wine and boil for 10 minutes to drive off most of the alcohol. Add the stock and remaining ingredients and return to a boil. Pour into the casserole.

Cover and cook in a preheated oven at 300°F for 3½–4 hours, until the meat is very tender and falling from the bone.

Remove the chops to a clean container. Pour the cooking liquid through a strainer and remove and discard the cinnamon sticks, bay leaves, thyme, and orange zest. Using the back of a wooden spoon, press the vegetables through the strainer and into the strained liquid. Mix well and pour over the chops. Let cool, then chill overnight.

The next day, skim off and discard the fat, then reheat thoroughly. Serve with mashed potatoes.

CASSEROLED LAMB SHANKS
with eggplant and tomato gratin

Serious comfort food. Braised lamb shanks can't be rushed, but you can cook them a day in advance. Then, once you've prepared the gratin, you will have a delicious meal in just over half an hour. I prefer them the next day because I can remove any excess fat from the dish before reheating.

Make small incisions all over the lamb with a knife. Stud with the garlic and half the basil leaves. Brush the shanks lightly with olive oil. Season.

Heat the oil in a large skillet, add the onions, celery, and carrots, and sauté until lightly browned. Transfer to a large, deep casserole. Add the lamb to the hot skillet and sear until browned on all sides. Put on top of the vegetables and tuck in the bay leaf and remaining basil.

Pour the wine into the pan, heat, and stir to dissolve the sticky sediment. Add to the casserole. Heat the stock, then add to the casserole.

Cover and cook in a preheated oven at 350°F for about 30 minutes, then reduce to 325°F and cook for a further 1½ hours or until the meat is tender. Remove the shanks, let cool, and chill overnight. Strain the cooking liquid and chill overnight. Discard the vegetables. The next day, remove the solidified fat from the liquid.

To make the eggplant and tomato gratin, heat 3 tablespoons of the oil in a skillet, add the onions, and sauté until lightly golden. Remove and set aside. Sauté the eggplant in the same way as the onions, then remove and drain.

Layer the onions, potatoes, and eggplants in a gratin dish, seasoning each layer and sprinkling with the olives. Top with the tomatoes. Season with salt and pepper and drizzle with the remaining oil.

Reheat the lamb cooking liquid until boiling and pour ⅔ cup over the gratin. Return the shanks to the casserole and add the remaining liquid. Cook both dishes in a preheated oven at 350°F for about 30-40 minutes until the vegetables are cooked and the lamb is heated through. Serve the lamb on top of the gratin and sprinkle with rosemary leaves.

4 lamb shanks, about 1 lb. each

2 garlic cloves, cut into slivers

a handful of fresh basil leaves

2 tablespoons olive oil, for cooking, plus extra for brushing

2 onions, skins on and thickly sliced

2 celery stalks, thickly sliced

2 carrots, unpeeled and thickly sliced

1 bay leaf

1 cup light red wine such as pinot noir

2 cups lamb stock

sea salt and freshly ground black pepper

EGGPLANT AND TOMATO GRATIN:

⅓ cup olive oil

2 red onions, finely sliced

3 thin eggplants, finely sliced and dried well

2 potatoes, par-boiled in salted water, then finely sliced

2 tablespoons black olives in oil, drained and pitted

8 plum tomatoes, thickly sliced

sea salt and freshly ground black pepper

rosemary sprigs, to serve

SERVES 4

Make small incisions all over the lamb with a sharp knife. Stud with the garlic and the leaves from one sprig of rosemary. Season the lamb.

Heat a cast-iron or heavy-bottom skillet until hot, add the lamb, and dry-fry on all sides to brown and seal in the juices. Remove and set aside.

Melt the butter in the hot skillet, add the shallots and sweet potatoes, and sauté, shaking the skillet from time to time, until the vegetables are lightly browned and coated in butter. Transfer to a large, shallow baking dish.

Put the wine in the skillet, add the bay leaf and the remaining rosemary sprig and bring to a boil. Stir in half the hot stock, then add to the vegetables. Top with the lamb.

Cook, uncovered, in a preheated oven at 350°F for 1½ hours until the lamb and vegetables are cooked, tender, and browned. Baste 2–3 times during cooking to keep everything moist and add extra stock or water, if necessary. When cooked, the lamb will be pink in the middle, but if you prefer it well done, return it to the oven (without the vegetables) for a further 20 minutes.

Transfer the lamb and vegetables to a heated serving platter, cover, and let the meat rest for about 5–10 minutes. Meanwhile, strain the cooking liquid into a pitcher, drop in a few ice cubes, and let stand until the fat rises to the top and starts to set. Spoon off and discard the fat.

Put the liquid in a saucepan and boil until reduced and slightly thickened. Beat in a few small cubes of butter, one at a time, until glossy and thick.

To serve, pour some of the sauce over the meat and vegetables and serve the rest separately.

3 lb. boneless shoulder of lamb, trimmed, rolled, and tied

2 garlic cloves, cut into slivers

2 sprigs of rosemary

2 tablespoons unsalted butter, plus extra for the sauce

24 baby shallots, or 8 large, peeled but left whole

3 medium sweet potatoes, cut into large cubes

1 cup dry white wine

1 bay leaf

2 cups hot lamb stock

sea salt and freshly ground black pepper

SERVES 4

Pot-roasting is easy. The meat is browned with the vegetables to add extra flavor, then stock and wine are added. It is left to open-roast to concentrate the juices and at the end you have a ready-made sauce. Make sure you baste the lamb from time to time as it cooks to keep it beautifully moist and rich in flavor.

POT-ROASTED LAMB
with rosemary and sweet potatoes

Toss the beef in the seasoned flour until coated. Set aside. Heat half the oil in a flameproof casserole, add the shallots, garlic, and pancetta or bacon, and sauté until lightly browned. Remove and set aside. Sauté the mushrooms in the bacon fat in the casserole, remove, and set aside.

Heat the remaining oil in the casserole, add the meat, and sauté until browned (cook in batches, if necessary). Remove and set aside. Pour ½ cup of the wine into the casserole and heat, stirring to deglaze the pan juices and sticky sediment.

Return the sautéed meat and vegetables to the casserole. Add the bouquet garni, tangerine peel, stock, and remaining wine. Bring to a boil.

Cover and cook in a preheated oven at 325°F for about 3-3½ hours until the meat is tender but juicy—the gelatinous parts will have melted to give a rich sauce.

To make the dumplings, sift the flour and baking powder into a bowl. Rub in the butter with your fingertips until it resembles breadcrumbs. Stir in the onion, thyme, salt, and pepper. Add the milk and stir in enough water, 1 tablespoon at a time, to make a very soft dough.

Remove the casserole from the oven and increase to 350°F. Drop tablespoons of the dumpling mixture into the casserole. Cover and return to the oven for 15-20 minutes until the dumplings are light and fluffy.

Remove and discard the peel and bouquet garni. Serve from the casserole, sprinkled with lots of freshly chopped parsley.

3 lb. shin of beef, cut into 2-inch cubes

2 tablespoons seasoned flour

¼ cup olive oil

30 baby shallots, peeled but left whole

1 fat garlic clove, crushed

½ cup chopped pancetta or bacon

2¼ cups button mushrooms

3 cups full-bodied red wine

1 fresh bouquet garni (2 bay leaves tied together with sprigs of thyme and parsley and a piece of celery)

dried peel of 1 tangerine*

3 cups beef stock

sea salt and freshly ground black pepper

chopped fresh parsley, to serve

HERB DUMPLINGS:

¾ cup self-rising flour

½ teaspoon baking powder

2 tablespoons unsalted butter

½ small onion, finely chopped

1 tablespoon fresh thyme leaves

2 tablespoons milk

sea salt and freshly ground black pepper

*__Note:__ *Available from Asian markets.*

SERVES 4

BRAISED TANGERINE BEEF with herb dumplings

Shin of beef is perfect for slow-cooking—it makes a rich, sticky, juicy gravy. It is also exceptional value for money. Let fresh tangerine peel dry out for a few days near a hot oven, then use it in the casserole; the citrus flavor of the beef sauce will intensify dramatically.

Rub 1 tablespoon of the oil over the beef and put in a large, deep dish. Break the ginger in half and crush one piece with a heavy knife to release the oils and flavor. Add to the beef. Peel the remaining ginger and slice into thin matchstick pieces. Set aside.

Cut the garlic head in half crosswise, then put it beside the meat and tuck in the thyme and bay leaves. Add the beef stock, half the wine, peppercorns, and 2 tablespoons of the oil. Cover and marinate in the refrigerator overnight, turning the meat from time to time.

Remove the meat from the marinade and pat dry with paper towels. Reserve the marinade. Heat a large, cast-iron or heavy-bottom skillet until hot, add the beef, and dry-fry until browned on all sides. Remove and spread the mustard evenly over the beef.

Heat the remaining oil in the skillet, add the onions, carrots, and celery, and sauté until slightly golden. Transfer to a large casserole. Add the reserved ginger matchsticks.

Strain the marinade into a saucepan and return the herbs and cut garlic to the casserole. Season. Heat the marinade until boiling.

Put the beef on top of the vegetables and pour over the hot marinade. Cover and cook in a preheated oven at 300°F for about 4–4½ hours until tender, turning and basting the meat 2–3 times during cooking. Remove from the oven, season, then return to the oven uncovered. Increase to 400°F and cook for 15 minutes until the outside of the meat is crisp. Remove the beef and keep it warm.

To make the sauce, add the remaining wine to the casserole and heat, stirring to dissolve the crusty sediment. Strain into a saucepan and, using the back of a wooden spoon, press the vegetables through the strainer and into the pan. Bring to a boil and beat in the butter, a little at a time, if using, until the sauce is thick and glossy. Season to taste.

Slice the beef and serve with the sauce poured over, roasted vegetables, and a sprinkling of chopped parsley.

¼ cup olive oil

5 lb. boned and rolled beef brisket

3 inches fresh ginger

1 whole head garlic, unpeeled

7–8 sprigs of thyme

4 bay leaves

1 cup beef stock

3 cup red wine

1 tablespoon crushed peppercorns

2 tablespoons mustard

2 red onions, coarsely chopped

2 carrots, unpeeled and coarsely chopped

2 celery stalks, coarsely chopped

2 tablespoons unsalted butter (optional)

sea salt and freshly ground black pepper

chopped fresh parsley, to serve

SERVES 4 as a main dish, then 4 the next day when cold

SLOW-COOKED BRISKET
marinated in red wine with ginger and garlic

Since there is less shrinkage in a larger piece of meat, it is worth cooking more than you need. When cold, the rest makes a wonderful sandwich filling or may be served with a salad.

Inspired by the flavors of the Caribbean, this dish is rib-stickingly delicious. Chiles come in all shapes, sizes, and colors—and varying degrees of heat. Usually the smaller the chile the hotter it is. The exception is the very hot Scotch bonnet or habanero. I've used a mild jalapeño here, but if you prefer a fiery sensation, use a hotter chile.

RUM and CHILE BEEF CASSEROLE
with oven-baked squash

Cut the steak into thick rounds and put in a deep, non-reactive dish. To make the marinade, mix all the ingredients together, add to the beef, and toss well to coat. Cover and marinate in the refrigerator overnight, turning the meat from time to time.

To make the oven-baked squash, heat the oil in a flameproof casserole, add the squash, nutmeg, salt, and pepper and sauté until lightly browned and coated in oil. Set aside.

Drain the beef and pat dry. Strain and reserve the marinade. Toss the meat in the seasoned flour until coated, then shake off excess flour.

Heat half the oil in a cast-iron or heavy-bottom skillet, add the meat (in batches), and sauté until browned on all sides. Transfer to a casserole.

Add the remaining oil to the skillet and sauté the onions, garlic, and chiles until softened and translucent. Season. Add to the casserole. Tuck in the bay leaves and oregano.

Put the reserved marinade and stock in the skillet and bring to a boil, stirring to de-glaze the pan juices. Pour over the beef. Cover and cook in a preheated oven at 350°F for 1 hour, then reduce to 300°F and cook for 1½–2 hours. Add the squash to the oven and cook both casseroles, uncovered, for about 40 minutes until the meat is tender and squash is cooked. Remove the bay leaves and oregano.

Sprinkle chives over the squash and serve with the meat and sauce. Add extra chiles, if using.

3 lb. chuck steak, trimmed

1 tablespoon seasoned flour

¼ cup olive oil

2 large onions

4 garlic cloves

2 red jalapeño chiles, seeded and finely sliced, plus extra for serving (optional)

2 bay leaves

3 sprigs of oregano

2 cups beef stock

sea salt and freshly ground black pepper

MARINADE:

2 red jalapeño chiles, seeded and sliced

finely grated zest and juice of 3 limes

1 cup dark rum

1 tablespoon dark soy sauce

2 tablespoons brown sugar

1 tablespoon crushed black peppercorns

4 bay leaves, torn in half

2–3 sprigs of oregano

OVEN-BAKED SQUASH:

¼ cup olive oil

1 butternut squash, peeled, seeded, and cut into cubes

a pinch of freshly grated nutmeg

salt and freshly ground black pepper

scissor-snipped chives, to serve

SERVES 4

8 cups vegetable stock

2¼ cups basmati rice, soaked in cold water overnight, drained, and rinsed

½ cup unsalted butter

1 onion, finely chopped

2 garlic cloves, crushed

1 small sprig of rosemary, chopped, plus extra to serve

⅔ cup dried apricots, cut into large pieces

⅓ cup shelled and peeled pistachio nuts

a large pinch of saffron threads

black seeds from 10 green cardamom pods, crushed

sea salt and freshly ground black pepper

TOMATO AND MUSHROOM SAUCE:

¼ cup olive oil

½ small onion, finely chopped

1 garlic clove, finely chopped

1 celery stalk, sliced

½ yellow bell pepper, seeded and diced

6 plum tomatoes, skinned, seeded, and diced

6 button mushrooms, sliced

sea salt and freshly ground black pepper

SERVES 4

PERSIAN RICE

A Middle Eastern dish, traditionally cooked on top of the stove. The rice is left to cook undisturbed so that a golden crust forms at the bottom of the pan, which then becomes the top when turned out. It's the prized part that everyone wants. This dish cooks well in the oven because you're less tempted to have a look at it or stir the rice, which would ruin the whole effect. Serve with a chunky tomato and mushroom sauce for a delicious meat-free supper.

Heat the stock and 1 tablespoon salt in a large saucepan until boiling. Add the rice, cook for about 4 minutes, then drain. Melt half the butter in a 6½-inch ovenproof saucepan, add the onion, garlic, and rosemary and sauté until the onion is softened but not browned.

Mix in the apricots, pistachios, saffron, and cardamom. Add the partially cooked rice and fork it through the mixture. Dot the surface with the remaining butter.

Stretch a clean, damp cloth over the top of the pan, cover with a lid, and bring the ends of the cloth up over the lid. Let steam in a preheated oven at 250°F for 45 minutes; do not remove the lid during cooking. Remove from the oven—the rice should be tender and moist.

To make the sauce, heat the oil in a skillet, add the onion, garlic, and celery, and sauté until softened. Add the remaining ingredients and cook for 5-6 minutes, until soft but still chunky.

To unmold the rice, run a spatula carefully around the pan and turn out on to a serving plate so the golden crust is on top. To serve, spoon the sauce around the rice and top with sprigs of rosemary.

VEGETABLES

Fresh oregano is used throughout the Mediterranean and gives this dish a warm, earthy flavor. If you can't get it, use flat-leaf parsley or chives instead. Flowering herbs look so beautiful and taste great too, so when in season, serve the vegetables with a sprinkling of purple oregano petals. They're delicious.

VEGETABLE TIAN
with mozzarella and oregano

Roast the bell peppers under a hot broiler or in a preheated oven at 400°F for 15-20 minutes or until the skins are charred and blackened. Put them in a plastic bag, seal, and let cool. Peel the peppers (the skin will come off easily), then cut them in half, and scrape out the seeds. Cut the flesh into thick strips. Set aside.

Heat the oil in a skillet, add the eggplant, and sauté briefly. Remove to a plate. In the same skillet, sauté the onions, zucchini, and garlic until just golden. Remove to a plate.

Add the wine and heat gently, stirring to de-glaze the pan juices.

Put the prepared vegetables and plum tomatoes in a shallow, ovenproof dish. Sprinkle with the olives and pour over the heated wine. Drizzle with the balsamic vinegar and sprinkle with half the oregano. Season with salt and freshly ground black pepper.

Bake at 400°F for 20 minutes. Remove from the oven, dot the top with the mozzarella and cook for a further 10-15 minutes or until the cheese has melted and the vegetables are well roasted.

Sprinkle with the remaining oregano and serve with crusty country bread to mop up the lovely juices.

2 yellow bell peppers

⅓ cup olive oil

1 long, thin eggplant, cut into thick slices

2 red onions, cut into quarters

2 medium zucchini, cut diagonally into chunks

12 garlic cloves

1 cup red wine

12 ripe plum tomatoes, cut in half lengthwise

12 black olives, pitted

2 tablespoons balsamic vinegar

1 tablespoon chopped fresh oregano

2 mozzarella cheeses, about 5 oz. each, drained and thickly sliced

sea salt and freshly ground black pepper

SERVES 4

Add the potatoes to a saucepan of boiling salted water and cook for 5 minutes. Drain and let cool for a few minutes.

Put a layer of potatoes in a greased 6-cup gratin dish and top with a layer of chopped onions. Add a few sage leaves, salt, and pepper. Repeat, finishing with a layer of potato.

Melt the butter in a skillet, add the apples, and turn to coat well. Arrange the apples on top of the potatoes, slightly overlapping each slice. Beat the cream and egg until mixed, then add the nutmeg, salt, and pepper, and pour over the apples.

Bake in a preheated oven at 375°F for about 50 minutes to 1 hour until the potatoes are tender—test by piercing the center with a skewer. Remove from the oven.

For a golden, nutty top, flash-cook the gratin under a hot broiler.

3 lb. waxy potatoes, finely sliced

1 onion, finely chopped

leaves from 3–4 sprigs of sage

1 tablespoon unsalted butter

4 Granny Smith apples, peeled and thickly sliced

1 cup heavy cream

1 egg

a large pinch of freshly grated nutmeg

sea salt and freshly ground black pepper

SERVES 4 as a main dish or 6 as an accompaniment

POTATO, SAGE, and APPLE GRATIN

Perfect for the busy cook, the vegetables can be layered ahead of time, then topped with the apples before baking. The gratin is delicious with any braised meat, especially pork, and particularly good with spicy sausages.

Peel and trim the vegetables, then cut into medium chunks, but leave the shallots whole.

Heat the butter in a large skillet, add the vegetables, and cook, stirring over a high heat until lightly browned. Season with salt and pepper.

Sprinkle with the sugar and cook until the vegetables are slightly caramelized. Tip into a casserole and add the chickpeas.

Add the stock, thyme, and bay leaf to the skillet and bring to a boil. Pour into the casserole, cover, and cook in a preheated oven at 300°F for 1 hour. Increase to 400°F and cook, uncovered, for about 15-20 minutes until the vegetables are tender and glazed and the cooking liquid has reduced slightly. Season to taste. Serve sprinkled with snipped chives.

1 celery root, about 1 lb.

3 carrots

4 leeks

2 parsnips

12 shallots

¼ cup unsalted butter

2 teaspoons brown sugar

¾ cup dried chickpeas, soaked overnight, then cooked unsalted until tender, or 14 oz. canned chickpeas, rinsed and drained

2 cups vegetable stock

4-5 sprigs of thyme

1 bay leaf, torn in half

sea salt and freshly ground black pepper

scissor-snipped chives, to serve

SERVES 4

Chickpeas add a nutty flavor and buttery texture. Sautéing the vegetables first will caramelize their natural sugars to give extra flavor. Serve with meat or crusty bread.

BRAISED ROOT VEGETABLES
with chickpeas and thyme

Put the beans in a large saucepan and cover with twice their volume of water. Bring to a boil, then simmer gently for 30 minutes or until the beans are tender. Drain and reserve about 2 cups of the cooking liquid.

To blanch the pork or bacon, put the meat in a saucepan and cover with cold water. Bring to a boil, then drain. Using a sharp knife, score fine cuts across the rind of the pork or bacon, then put the pieces into a casserole.

Melt the butter in a large skillet, add the onions, and sauté until golden. Stir in the mustard, molasses, and sugar. Add the reserved liquid and salt. Mix in the beans, passata or chopped tomatoes, and oregano or marjoram, and pour over the bacon or pork. Cover and cook in a preheated oven at 300°F for 3 hours or until the meat is cooked and rind is crisp. Check during cooking and if the beans have absorbed too much liquid, add boiling water. Add the Worcestershire sauce and lemon juice, if using. Keep the casserole warm.

For the glazed carrots, heat a heavy-bottom roasting pan on top of the stove and, when hot, add the butter, oil, and carrots. Turn the carrots until well coated. Add the honey and salt and mix well. Roast in a preheated oven at 425°F for about 10 minutes, stirring halfway through cooking. Sprinkle with the sesame seeds and return to the oven for a further 5-6 minutes until the carrots are cooked, golden, and crisp. Reheat the baked beans, if necessary, and serve with the glazed carrots.

2 cups dried navy beans, soaked overnight in cold water to cover, then drained

1 lb. piece salt pork or slab bacon, cut in half

1/4 cup unsalted butter

2 onions, finely chopped

2 teaspoons dry mustard

3 tablespoons molasses

1/4 cup brown sugar

1 cup passata or 14 oz. canned chopped plum tomatoes

3-4 sprigs of oregano or marjoram

1 tablespoon Worcestershire sauce (optional)

1 tablespoon freshly squeezed lemon juice (optional)

sea salt and freshly ground black pepper

HONEY and SESAME GLAZED CARROTS:

1/4 cup unsalted butter

2 tablespoons olive oil

6 large carrots, cut into chunks

1 tablespoon honey

2 tablespoons sesame seeds

sea salt

SERVES 4

The distinctive flavor of this famous dish comes•from the salt pork. My grandmother used to make it with pork hock and molasses. Great Northern beans, flageolets, or small white beans are wonderful cooked this way too. If you are vegetarian, leave out the meat and halve the cooking time—when cooked, add a tablespoon of soy sauce and a swirl of olive oil to make up for the lost flavor.

BOSTON BAKED BEANS
with honey and sesame glazed carrots

4 parsnips

1 butternut squash, seeded

¼ cup olive oil

1 small onion, finely chopped

1 garlic clove, finely chopped

1¾ cups unsweetened coconut milk

⅔ cup heavy cream

a pinch of sugar

⅓ cup walnut halves

salt and freshly ground mixed peppercorns

fresh cilantro leaves, to serve

CURRY SPICE MIX:

1½ tablespoons cumin seeds

1 tablespoon coriander seeds

1–2 teaspoons caraway seeds

black seeds from 4 green cardamom pods, crushed

2 star anise

½ tablespoon fenugreek seeds

½ teaspoon freshly grated nutmeg

1 tablespoon mild curry powder

1 garlic clove, crushed

olive oil, for binding

SERVES 4

You won't need all of the curry spice mix for this dish and what you don't use can be put into a screw-top jar and refrigerated. It is wonderful added to sauces, marinades, or rubbed onto fish or meat before cooking.

CURRIED PARSNIPS and SQUASH with walnuts

To make the curry mix, grind the spice seeds and star anise to a powder in a spice mill or coffee grinder. Put in a bowl and add the curry powder and garlic. Mix in enough olive oil to make a paste.

Cut the parsnips and squash into even-sized pieces. Heat half the oil in a skillet, add the vegetables, and toss quickly to coat. Season lightly, then transfer to an ovenproof dish.

In the same skillet, heat the remaining oil and sauté the onion and garlic until soft. Add 1 tablespoon of the curry paste and cook to release the aromas. Add the coconut milk and cream. Season lightly and add the sugar. Heat gently, then pour the sauce over the vegetables.

Cover with foil and cook in a preheated oven at 350°F for about 45 minutes or until the vegetables are tender.

Remove from the oven and sprinkle with the walnuts. Return to the oven and cook, uncovered, for about 15–20 minutes, until the vegetables are golden and the sauce has caramelized slightly. Serve with cilantro.

2 tablespoons unsalted butter

1 tablespoon sugar, plus extra
for dusting

1/2 cup risotto rice, such as arborio
or carnaroli

2 cups milk

1 cup light cream

1 strip of lemon zest

a pinch of salt

1 vanilla bean, split in half
lengthwise

4 thick slices of fresh pineapple

2 bananas

confectioners' sugar, for dusting

8 wooden skewers, soaked in water
for 20 minutes

SERVES 4

Put the butter and sugar into a saucepan and heat until foaming. Stir in the rice, coating the grains until they glisten. In another pan, boil the milk until frothing, then gradually add to the rice, stirring. Add the cream, lemon zest, and salt.

Scrape the seeds from the vanilla bean into the rice mixture, then add the bean. Heat until almost boiling, then pour into a deep, ovenproof dish. Cover with parchment paper to prevent a brown skin forming on the top. Bake in a preheated oven at 275°F for about 2–2½ hours until creamy and thick.

Remove from the oven and take out the lemon zest and vanilla bean.

Spoon the pudding into 4 large ramekins and let cool until lukewarm.

Cut the pineapple and bananas into chunks and push onto the skewers. Sift confectioners' sugar onto the skewered fruit and put under a hot broiler until the sugar has caramelized. Let cool.

Dust the puddings with a thick layer of confectioners' sugar and sugar and caramelize as before. Let cool until set, then serve with the fruit skewers.

The quintessential nursery dessert, and the definitive comfort food. It's very simple to make and when served like this, with a caramelized sugar top, it is sophisticated enough for even the smartest dinner party.

RICE PUDDING
with caramelized pineapple and banana

DESSERTS

8 firm pears, peeled and cored but left whole

1½ cups red wine

3 cups ruby port

1 tablespoon juniper berries, about 20 berries, crushed

zest of 1 lemon, cut in a long strip

¼ cup sugar

6 pieces crystallized ginger, finely diced

3 teaspoons arrowroot, blended with 2 tablespoons of port

TO SERVE:

1 cup crème fraîche

1 tablespoon superfine sugar

finely grated zest of ½ lemon

SERVES 8

Simple to make yet stunningly beautiful. Choose well-shaped pears—ripe but still very firm, so they hold their form during cooking. I like the pears hot or cold, served with lots of lemon crème fraîche or ginger or lemon ice cream.

PEARS in PORT
with juniper and ginger

Stand the pears upright in a deep, ovenproof dish. Put the wine, port, juniper berries, lemon zest, and sugar in a saucepan and bring to a boil, stirring until the sugar dissolves. Pour the mixture over the pears to cover. Stir in the ginger.

Cover and bake in a preheated oven at 300°F for 45 minutes to 1 hour or until the pears are very tender (depending on ripeness). Baste them 2–3 times during cooking.

Remove from the oven and, using a slotted spoon, transfer the pears to a deep bowl.

Pour the cooking liquid into a saucepan and stir in the blended arrowroot until mixed. Bring to a boil, stirring until the wine syrup is smooth and slightly thickened. Remove and discard the lemon zest, then pour the wine syrup over the pears. Serve immediately or chill overnight: the pears will turn a deep purple-red and the spiced wine flavor will intensify dramatically.

To serve, mix the crème fraîche, sugar, and lemon zest until blended. Add spoonfuls of the mixture to the pears and drizzle over the wine syrup.

Delicious with clotted cream or a dollop of crème fraîche. This simple dessert reminds me of Christmas with its spicy aromas and mulled-wine flavors. Soak the dried fruit until they are plump, according to the package instructions, before using them in this dish.

MULLED FRUIT COMPOTE
with cinnamon and cloves

2½ –3 cups mixed dried fruits, such as figs, apricots, prunes, and apple rings, rinsed and drained

2 teaspoons arrowroot

3 cups dry red wine, such as Rhône

1 cup Madeira wine

10 allspice berries, crushed

5 whole cloves

1 cinnamon stick

1 long strip of orange zest

1 long strip of lemon zest

freshly squeezed juice of 1 lemon, plus extra if necessary

3 tablespoons brown sugar

¾ cup fresh blueberries

TO SERVE:

orange zest, finely sliced

lemon zest, finely sliced

sugar, for tossing

SERVES 4–6

Put the dried fruits in a casserole. Mix the arrowroot with 2 tablespoons of the wine. Pour the remaining wine and Madeira into a large saucepan and add the spices, citrus zests, lemon juice, and sugar. Heat until the sugar has dissolved and the mixture is boiling. Add a little of the spiced wine to the blended arrowroot, stir until smooth, then pour back into the pan. Heat, stirring, until slightly thickened.

Pour over the dried fruits, cover tightly with a lid or foil and bake in a preheated oven at 300°F for about 2 hours until the fruits are plump and the liquid is syrupy.

Remove and discard the strips of zest and cinnamon stick. Add extra lemon juice, if the compote is too sweet. Add the blueberries, let cool, then chill. To serve, toss the finely sliced orange and lemon zest in sugar and sprinkle on top of the compote.

Slow-cooked until velvety smooth, this tangy dessert is heavenly. Cooking the cream in individual ramekins is also simple—and takes half the time of the large one. If you do it like this, caramelize and serve it in the ramekins.

LEMON CREAM with praline crisps

10 medium eggs

2 cups sugar

finely grated zest and juice of 8 unwaxed lemons

2 cups heavy cream

confectioners' sugar, for dusting

PRALINE CRISPS:

¼ cup sugar

6 hazelnuts, roasted and skinned

a 3-inch plain cookie cutter

SERVES 6

To make the praline crisps, put the sugar and 2 tablespoons water in a small saucepan. Bring to a boil, stirring until the sugar dissolves and turns to a light caramel.

Put the hazelnuts on a greased baking sheet and pour over the hot caramel. Let set. Break into pieces and process to a powder in a food processor. Turn out onto a baking sheet lined with parchment paper and spread thinly to form a large rectangle.

Bake in a preheated oven at 350°F for 2–3 minutes until melted. Remove from the oven and let cool for a few minutes. Using a sharp knife, score triangles in the praline. Let set.

To make the lemon cream, beat the eggs and half the sugar in a large bowl. Add the lemon zest and juice and beat until mixed.

Put the cream and remaining sugar in a saucepan, bring to a boil, and pour over the egg mixture, beating as you pour. Chill overnight to let the flavors develop.

When ready to cook, pass the lemon cream through a fine strainer into a 12 x 7½ x 1½ inch baking dish. Put in a roasting pan filled halfway with water and bake in a preheated oven at 250°F for about 1 hour or until just set but still slightly wobbly in the middle.

Remove from the oven and let cool until firm. Using a 3-inch plain cookie cutter, press out 6 rounds. Carefully lift each one out of the baking dish and put on a plate. (Reserve the trimmings to serve another day with fruit.)

Sift a thick layer of confectioners' sugar over the top of each lemon cream, then caramelize until crisp and golden under a hot broiler.

To serve, carefully lift off the praline triangles and lean them against the lemon cream.

INDEX